When music sounds, gone is the earth I know,
And all her lovely things even lovelier grow;
Her flowers in vision flame, her forest trees
Lift burdened branches, stilled with ecstasies

When music sounds, out of the water rise
Naiads whose beauty dims my waking eyes,
Rapt in strange dreams burns each enchanted face,
With solemn echoing stirs their dwelling place.

WALTER DE LA MARE

MEETINGS WITH THE Fairies

MEETINGS WITH THE
Fairies

ELIZABETH RATISSEAU

LAUGHING ELEPHANT   MM11

ALL RIGHTS RESERVED   FIRST PRINTING
PRINTED IN SINGAPORE
ISBN 1-883211-56-5

LAUGHING ELEPHANT
3645 INTERLAKE AVENUE NORTH
SEATTLE WASHINGTON 98103
1-800-354-0400

WWW.LAUGHINGELEPHANT.COM

Which is the road to Fairyland?
　Over the hills and far away,
　But you mustn't go till the end of the day,
　When the sun is red and the trees are still,
　All good little children dance over the hill,
　Where the fairies are waiting to take their hand
　And show them the footpath to fairyland.

EUNICE CLOSE

In the old time every Wood and Grove, Field and Meadow, Hill and Cave, Sea and River, was tenanted by tribes and communities of the great Fairy Family, and at least one of its members was a resident in every House and Homestead where the kindly virtues of charity and hospitality were practiced and cherished. This was the faith of our forefathers—a graceful trustful faith, peopling the whole earth with beings whose mission was to watch over and protect all helpless and innocent things; to encourage the good, to comfort the forlorn, to punish the wicked, and to thwart and subdue the overbearing.

ARCHIBALD MACLAREN

From the earliest ages the world has believed in the existence of a race midway between the angel and man, gifted with power to exercise a strange mysterious influence over human destiny. The Persians called this mystic race Peris; the Egyptians and the Greeks named them demons, not as evil, but as mysterious allies of man, invisible though ever present; capable of kind acts but implacable if offended.

LADY WILDE

A little north of the town of Sligo… some hundreds of feet above the plain is a small white square in the limestone. No mortal has ever touched it … There is no more inaccessible place upon the earth and few more encircled by awe … It is the door of faery-land. In the middle of night it swings open, and the unearthly troop rushes out. All night the gay rabble sweep to and fro across the land, invisible to all.

W.B. YEATS

Did in the gardins of Adonis fynd
A goodly creature, whom he deemed in mynd
To be no earthly wight, but either spright
Of angell, the authour of all woman-kynd;
There a Fay he her according hight,
Of whom all Faryes spring and fetch there
lignage right.

Of these a mighty people shortly grew,
And puissant kings, which all the world warrayd,
And to themselves all nations did subdue.

EDMUND SPENSER

Far from being outdated, quaint or romantically obscure, the faery tradition is coming back. As an open secret, it has already had a huge revival. What is our greening concern with the environment but a 21st century restatement of the faery truth, taught by the old Gaelic seers, that all living creatures are interwoven, living upon and within one another?

R. J. STEWART

Faërie cannot be caught in a net of words; for it is one of its qualities to be indescribable, though not imperceptible.

J.R.R. TOLKIEN

I believe when I am in the mood that nature is full of people whom we cannot see, and that some of these are ugly or grotesque, and some wicked or foolish, but very many beautiful beyond any one we have ever seen, and that these are not far away ... the simple of all times and the wise men of ancient times have seen them and even spoken to them.

W.B. YEATS

The Fairy Market could often be seen in the distance. Like one kind of apparition these fairies were perceptible to only one sense at a time. They could be seen from a distance, a crowd of brightly-dressed people chaffering on a green hillside, but when the spectator approached he could see nothing, only felt himself pressed, squeezed and jostled by an invisible crowd.

RICHARD BOVET

Time in fairyland passes very rapidly … Stories of this different pulse of fairy time comes to us from all over the kingdom and from most countries where there are any fairies at all. There is also a fairy or angelic bird, whose singing so enraptures the listener that a hundred years passes as he listens. The question arises of what happens to him while he listens, for he is invisible to humanity while he stands there and unaffected by anything that is happening in the place from which he yet seems never to have moved.

K.M. BRIGGS

Thus Launfal, withouten fable,
That noble night of the roundè table,
    Was taken into the faërie;
Since saw him in this land no man,
Ne no more of him tell I ne can,
    For soothe, without lie.

THOMAS CHESTRE

With astonishment I saw what she was seeing—a little figure about six inches high, in the perfect shape of a woman and with brilliantly colored diaphanous wings resembling those of a dragonfly. The figure held a little wand and was pointing it at the heart of a rose. At the top of the wand there was a little light, like a star. The figure's limbs were a very pale pink and visible through her clothes. She had long silver hair which resembled an aura. She hovered near the rose for at least two minutes, her wings vibrating rapidly like those of a hummingbird, and then she disappeared.

CYNTHIA MONTEFIORE

I was walking alone in my garden, there was a great stillness among the branches and flowers, and more than common sweetness in the air; I heard low and pleasant sound, and I know not whence it came. At last I saw the broad leaf of a flower move, and underneath I saw a procession of creatures the size and color of green and gray grasshoppers, bearing a body laid out on a rose-leaf, which they buried with songs and disappeared. It was a fairy funeral.

WILLIAM BLAKE

In a utilitarian age ... it is a matter of grave
importance that Fairy tales should be respected
... A nation without fancy, without some
romance, never did, never can, never will hold a
great place under the sun.

CHARLES DICKENS

O, then, I see Queen Mab hath been with you.
She is the fairies' midwife, and she comes
In shape no bigger than an agate-stone
On the fore-finger of an alderman,
Drawn with a team of little atomies
Athwart men's noses as they lie asleep;

And in this state she gallops night by night
Through lovers' brains, and then they dream of love;
O'er courtiers' knees, that dream on court'sies
straight,
O'er lawyers' fingers, who straight dream on fees,
O'er ladies ' lips, who straight on kisses dream,

WILLIAM SHAKESPEARE

An Irishman, upon seeing a four foot tall fairy, was told: "I am bigger than I appear to you now.
We can make the old young, the big small, the small big."

W.Y. EVANS WENTZ

Up the airy mountain
Down the rushy glen
We dare not go a-hunting
For fear of little men

WILLIAM ALLINGHAM

Gnomes ... are very loose-limbed and move with long prancing strides, though it is evident that they can also travel through the air with great speed, and I see some moving in this way, just skimming the ground ... Certainly the earth is not solid to them, as some of them are moving with their ankles and feet below the surface, without obstruction.

GEOFFREY HODSON

'Tis merry, 'tis merry in Fairy-land,
When fairy birds are singing,
When the court doth ride by their monarch's side,
With bit and bridle ringing.

WALTER SCOTT

Such a soft gloating witchery of sound
As twilight Elfins make, when they at eve
Voyage on gentle gales from Fairy-Land

SAMUEL COLERIDGE

Thomas Learmont of Ercildoune was sitting on
Huntly Bank to listen to the birds' song when he saw
a lady riding towards him of more than mortal beauty. She was dressed in green and her horse's mane
was hung with tinkling bells. She was so beautiful
that he took her to be the Queen of Heaven, but she told him frankly that she was no more than the Queen
of Elfland, and that one kiss of his lips on hers would put him in her power. In spite of that he kissed her glad-
ly, and became her bondman for seven years … the Queen of Elfland plucked an apple of truth from a tree
and gave it to Thomas, with the gift of prophecy. And from that hour on Thomas could speak nothing but the
truth, and in fairyland and the mortal world alike he went by the name of True Thomas.

WALTER SCOTT

They may take strange
Forms, but never say
They can't be seen–
Only they have a way
Of rearranging things,
Of fitting together
Cold lily-silver
Bodies and dark-netted
Dragonfly wings,

VALERIE WORTH

A little mushroom table spread,
After short prayers, they set on bread;
A moon-parcht grain of purest wheat,
With some small glit'ring gritt, to eate
His choice bits with; then in a tree
They make a feast lesse great than nice.

ROBERT HERRICK

Leap, fox; hoot, owl; wail, warbler sweet,
'Tis midnight now's a-brewing;
The fairy mob is all abroad,
And witches at their wooing.

WALTER DE LA MARE

Brownies vary in build: some tribes being short and squat, with fat, round bodies and short limbs; others being slim and youthful in appearance. Their height varies from four inches to a foot.

GEOFFREY HODSON

O hark, O hear! How thin and clear,
    And thinner, clearer, farther going!
O sweet and far from cliff and scar
    The horns of Elfland faintly blowing!

ALFRED TENNYSON

And many a time she came, and always it was good advice she was giving to my mother, and warning her what not to do if she would have good luck. There was none of the other children of us ever seen her unless me; but I used to be glad when I seen her coming up the burn, and would run out and catch her by the hand and the cloak, and call to my mother, "Here's the Wee Woman!" No man body ever seen her.

as told to W.B. YEATS

A little fairy dances
In every one I blow.
It isn't just a game to me,
A play-pretending game to me—
I've seen them, and I know.

ELIZA WYNKOOP

If once we see the world from the fairy point of view, we get a glimpse of a new universe. So many things which matter very much to us do not seem to matter at all to them. Life and death, for instance, are things which they know all about; to them there is no uncertainly and no tragedy involved … Fairies actually see the flow of life through all things. We live in a world of form without understanding the life force beneath the forms … Why do not most people see fairies? They live in the same world as we do, but their bodies are less dense than ours, though only slightly less dense than a tenuous gas. I feel sure that the veil between us and them is exceedingly thin—so thin that nearly anyone could penetrate it with a little effort along the right line. The difficulty is to indicate this line … A special sense must be awakened in people if they are to see fairies … They cannot be touched, or felt, yet they can certainly be seen.

DORA VAN GELDER

Since ever and ever the world began
 They have danced like a ribbon of flame,
They have sung their song through the centuries long
 And yet it is never the same.
And though you be foolish or though you be wise,
 With hair of silver or gold,
You could never be young as the fairies are,
 And never as old.

ROSE FYLEMAN

Children born of fairy stock
Never need for shirt or frock,
Never want for food or fire,
Always get their heart's desire:
Jingle pockets full of gold,
Marry when they're seven years old.
Every fairy child may keep
Two strong ponies and ten sheep;
All have houses, each his own,
Built of brick or granite stone;
They live on cherries, they run wild—
I'd love to be a Fairy's child

ROBERT GRAVES

An old woman, who was bed-ridden, was much entertained by the visits of the fairies, who played about all over the room, climbed up her bed and danced on the counterpane. Words failed her to describe the airs and graces of the fairy women, or their sauciness to the fairy men.

R. HUNT

Camping alone on Mount Shasta, at twilight, Karen Maralee heard singing, and in a clearing she saw "eleven tiny blue fairies, perhaps one foot tall, and seemingly transparent ... The blue color was electric, seeming to pulsate or flicker ... The wings were larger than the fairy bodies themselves were larger than the fairy bodies themselves and appeared to be particularly delicate and lacy."

I am off down the road

Where the fairy lanterns glowed

And the little pretty flitter-mice are flying:

A slender band of gray

It runs creepily away

And the hedges and the grasses are a-sighing.

The air is full of wings,

And of blundery beetle-things

That warn you with their whirring and their humming.

J.R.R. TOLKIEN

Oh, who is so merry, so merry, heigh ho!

As the lighthearted fairy? Heigh ho,

    Heigh ho!

    He dances and sings

    To the sounds of his wings

With a hey and a heigh and a ho!

ANONYMOUS

Mid-world ... is full of strange and beautiful forms appearing and vanishing ever about the mystic adventurer, and there are to be seen many beings such as the bards told of: Beings riding ... upon winged steeds, or surrounded ... with many colored birds, and why these images of beauty and mystery should be there I do not know, but they have entered into the imagination of poets in the past and have entered into the imagination of others who are still living.

GEORGE WILLIAM RUSSELL

"You will always remain a child, you will never grow old, you will never die. You just lie down and get to sleep for awhile. The sun will soon rise again over the fir-tops, the new day will soon look in through the window, you will soon see much clearer than you ever saw by the light of that tallow candle." "I must be off. Good bye to you, dreamer, and well met!" "Well met little goblin!"

AXEL MUNTHE

My name? Who needs a name that is a wanderer? Maybe if I come again, you will not know me—until I am gone again. It is said the Fables are of my kind, and that my mother was a Dreamer. An ancient family. Older than Babylon: older than Tyre. It is said that a forbear of mine was wont to sit under the blossoming of the Tree of Life and to play on his bassoon in the garden of Eden. His name, Mammazella, was Romance.

WALTER DE LA MARE

Cover   Eleanor Fortescue-Brickdale. "The Lover's World," 1905.

Endpapers   Richard Doyle. "The Fairy Tree," n.d.

Half-Title   Unknown. "Fairy Music," n.d.

Frontispiece   Eleanor Fortescue-Brickdale. "The Introduction," n.d.

Copyright   L.M. Deal. From *Elson-Gray Basic Readers: Book Three*, 1931.

1   William Holmes Sullivan. "The Bewitched Piper," 1882.

2   John Anster Fitzgerald. "The Land of Nod," n.d.

3   P.B. Hickling. "The Fairies' Song," n.d.

4   H. Koberstein. "Gnome et princesse," postcard, n.d.

5   Daniel Maclise. "Undine," 1844.

6   Edwin Landseer. "Titania and Bottom," c. 1851.

7   Arthur Rackham. From *The Tempest*, 1908.

8   Maria L. Kirk. From *Mopsa The Fairy*, 1910.

9   Edmund Dulac. From *Edmund Dulac's Picture-Book for the French Red Cross*, 1915.

10   John Anster Fitzgerald. "The Artist's Dream" 1857.

11   F. Aveline. "The Funeral March of a Bumble Bee," sheet music illustration, n.d.

12   John Duncan. "Merlin and the Fairy Queen," n.d.

13   George Cruikshank. "Queen Mab," n.d.

14   C.E. Brock. From *The Rain Children*, 1910.

15   Florence Anderson. From *My Fairyland: A Child's Own Visions*, c. 1910

16   Jessie Willcox Smith. "Cinderella and the Glass Slipper," 1916.

17   Henry Rheam. "The Fairy Wood," n.d.

18   Margaret Tarrant. From *The Book of the Clock*, 1920.

19   Ruth Mary Hallock. From *A Child's Garden of Verses*, 1919.

PRINCIPAL SOURCES

Janet Bord. Fairies: Real Encounters With Little People. New York: Carroll & Graf, 1997.

K.M. Briggs. The Personnel of Fairyland. Detroit: Singing Tree Press, 1971.

R.J. Stewart. The Living World of Faery. Glastonbury: Gothic Image Publications, 1995.

Dora van Gelder. The Real World of Fairies. Wheaton, IL: The Theosophical Publishing House, 1977.

W.B. Yeats. The Celtic Twilight. London: Lawrence and Bullen, 1893.